WINDOW STICKERS
HALLOWEEN

Dare to turn over each new page
and enter a world of spook-tastic activities!
Then press out the card pages to
create some Halloween crafts.

HOW TO USE YOUR GEL STICKERS:

1

2

3

Gently peel the
gel stickers from
the backing sheet.

~~Press~~ the gel stickers
on a ~~window~~ to create
your own creepy scene.

Peel off and move
the gel stickers to make
a new scene every time!

make
believe
ideas

D0752113

VAMPIRE WATCH

Draw lines to match the
vampires to their shadows.

HIDE-AND-SPOOK

How many pink monsters can you see hiding
in the haunted house? Write the answer.

....

3

THE DEEP DARK WOODS

Find and circle ten differences
between the scenes.

Check the boxes when you find them.

1 2 3 4 5 6 7 8 9 10

SCARY SWAMP
Color the zombie swamp.

Circle ten
blue flowers.

6

Find the zombie that looks like this.

DON'T GET CAUGHT!

Help the fly escape the spiderweb
before getting caught!

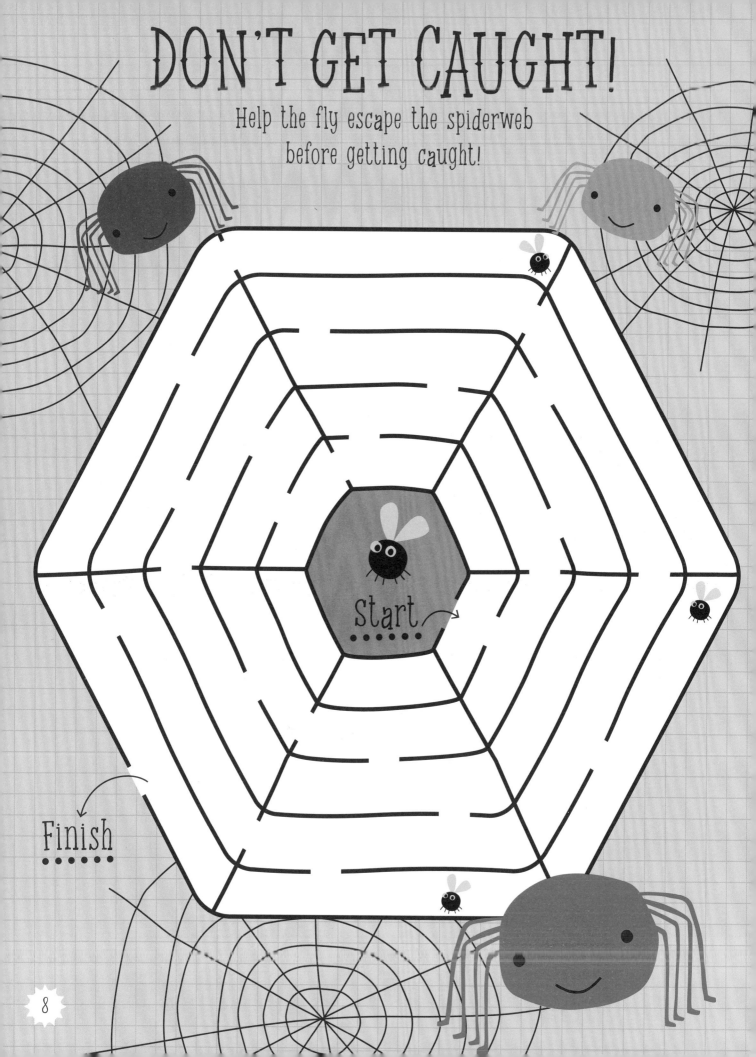

Start

Finish

8

CANDY COUNT

Search the grid for the patterns below.
Check the boxes when you find them.

TOMB ESCAPE

Finish the pyramid by writing the answers in the bricks.
Each brick is the total of the two numbers beneath it.

Find a path through the tomb.

Start →

Finish

Use color to finish the patterns.

Circle five differences between the mummies.

11

SCHOOL OF HORRORS

Circle **true** for the things that are in the picture.
Circle **false** for the things that are not in the picture.

There are two ghosts. True False

There are more wolves than witches. True False

There is only one moon. True False

KNOCK, KNOCK

Draw lines to match the jokes to the answers.

What do birds say on Halloween?

Because they have no-BODY to go with!

Why are ghosts bad liars?

SPELL-ing!

What is a witch's favorite subject?

Trick or TWEET!

Why don't skeletons like parties?

Because you can SEE THROUGH them!

HAUNTED HOUSE

Search the house for the things below.

How many can you see?
Write the answers in the circles.

4 cats

skeletons

pumpkins

.... bats   .... ghosts   .... spiders

15

TRICK OR TREAT?

Guide the trick-or-treater through the maze to the bag of treats. Use the key to guide you.

Key: → ↓ ← ↑

Start

Finish

MONSTER MATH

Draw a line from each sum
to the monster with the answer.

9

1

8

5 + 2

1 + 8

6

2

7

4 + 4

7 + 3

2 + 3

4

10

5

ALL HALLOWS' EVE
Color the picture. Use the key to guide you.

WHICH WITCH?

Follow the lines to find each witch's missing friend.
Write the letter next to each witch.

A   B   C

GHASTLY GARDEN

Use color to finish the patterns.

Circle five toads hiding on the page.

PETRIFYING PARADE

Guide the parade through the streets
by moving between the houses.
Follow the direction of the arrows.

Start

Finish

22

Doodle and color to finish the spooky lanterns.

Are there more zombies or people in the crowd?

.... zombies

.... people

WICKED WORDS

Find all the words in the chain of candy.
Write the words in the space below.

s p o o k y g h o s t v a
m
p
i
r
e
t
r
e
a
t
m
o
n s t e r z o m b i e

1	spooky	4	
2		5	
3		6	

Answer for page 25: 02

HIDDEN HOWLER

Solve the clues to reveal Luna's best friend.

Clue 1	Clue 2	Clue 3
They are standing in moonlight.	They have a tail.	They are holding a blue flower.

Remus

Elena

Jacob

Leah

Marcus

Nina

Oz

Rose

Seth

Who is Luna's best friend? Write the answer. _____

BEASTLY BAKES

Look at the recipe to see how to make one cupcake. How many cupcakes can you make with the pieces below?

Cupcake recipe

You will need:

1 liner

1 cake

1 topping

Write the answer. ....

Circle the thing that doesn't belong on each shelf.

Color the cookies and add spooky designs.

Answer for page 26: 5

DAY OF THE DEAD

Decorate the skull with
pretty doodles and bright colors.

28

PUMPKIN PATCH

How many pumpkins are growing
in the patch? Write the answer.

....

Draw a pumpkin. Use the grid to guide you.

CREEPY QUIZ

Look at the pictures to answer the questions below.

Who is upside down?

Who is making a potion?

Who is biggest?

Which monster is green and yellow?

Who is eating a taffy apple?

Who is sleeping?

MONSTER MASH

1 Pick a monster shape from the list.

2 Draw your monster into the space below and finish it with crazy colors, spikes, fangs, or even wings!

HAUNTED HOUSE

Press out the haunted house and stands.
Slot the house into the stands to finish.

TIP!
....
Press out the windows
and open the front door
to bring it to life!

HALLOWEEN FRIENDS

Press out the characters and stands. Slot the characters
into the stands or fold along the crease to make them stand up.
Then add them to your haunted house scene.

PUMPKIN PATCH

1. Press out the pumpkin patch and open the slots.
2. Then press out the pumpkin faces and fold along the crease, carefully opening the mouths.
3. Slide the pumpkin faces onto the pumpkin patch. Mix-and-match to make gruesome combos!

MONSTER MAKES

1. Press out shape A and shape B and open the slots.
2. Roll shape A into a tube and tape it together. Then slot shape B on top to finish.
3. Repeat step 1 and 2 with shapes C and D!

A

tape here

B

C

D

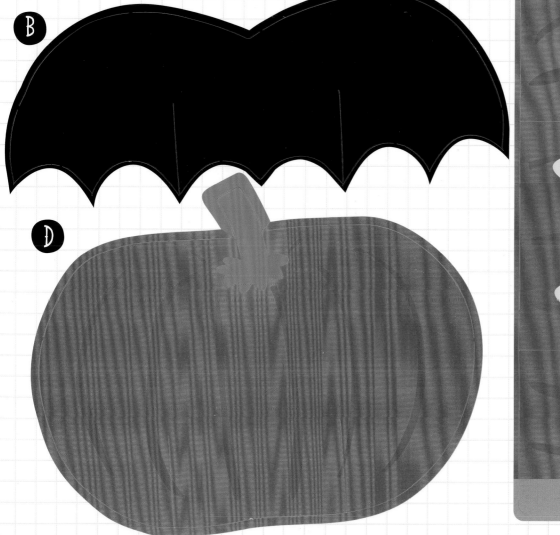

tape here